[handwritten notes]

ARMS: mod. to sides
(1) (8) (9)

TRUNK: (↓ Σ ↓ ↑↓)
mod. (9)

HIPS: ↗ + grip to one side
(5)

LEGS: ↦ mod (4)
↳ (9)

WARNING

This book is presented only as a means of preserving a unique aspect of the heritage of the martial arts. Neither Ohara Publications nor the author makes any representation, warranty or guarantee that the techniques described or illustrated in this book will be safe or effective in any self-defense situation or otherwise. You may be injured if you apply or train in the techniques of self-defense illustrated in this book, and neither Ohara Publications nor the author is responsible for any such injury that may result. It is essential that you consult a physician regarding whether or not to attempt any technique described in this book. Specific self-defense responses illustrated in this book may not be justified in any particular situation in view of all of the circumstances or under the applicable federal, state or local law. Neither Ohara Publications nor the author makes any representation or warranty regarding the legality or appropriateness of any technique mentioned in this book.

TAI·CHI CHUAN

by Marshall Ho'o

Editor: Mike Lee
Art Director: Sergio Onaga
Photography: Duwayne Uyehara and Art Foxall
Additional Photography: Sergio Onaga

Library of Congress Catalog Card Number: 86-51059
ISBN: 0-89750-109-8

OHARA 🔲 PUBLICATIONS, INCORPORATED
1813 Victory Place, P.O. Box 7728, Burbank, California 91510-7728

Acknowledgements

I wish to thank Mark Lambert, Strawberry Gatts, and Terry Case. Without their assistance this book would not have been possible.

I also wish to express my gratitude to Victoria Mallory who appears with me in the photos of this book. She is a highly accomplished actress whose tai chi is sheer perfection.

Dedication

This book is dedicated to Jill, Godonna, Brian, Galen, Maya, China, Taiping, Tola, Lincoln and to Wen Shan Huang, father of tai chi chuan in America.

Preface

The following is an effective short course in tai chi chuan intended for the complete novice. It is written so that the reader is not overwhelmed by the multifaceted nature of the art.

Tai chi chuan is a vast subject with a history reaching back centuries into the realms of legend, with techniques which take years to perfect and with cultural ramifications that are difficult to fathom for even the finest academic minds.

This book is meant to be read while hanging onto a strap in the bus, that is, as a primer for the busy person who finds that his spare time must be carefully allotted and who thinks that this art may have something to offer, as an exercise for his body, as a method of relaxing his mind, as a way of reacquainting himself with his own sense of spiritual balance. For now, he's just checking it out. If it works for him, he'll go on to dedicate more time to practice.

This book is also for the martial artist who is perhaps involved in the study of another style of martial arts. He has heard of, or seen tai chi chuan and would like to investigate its benefits. This reader will find tai chi chuan the perfect complement, heightening his energy, invigorating his health, and instilling the fundamentals of powerful body movement.

Still, the reader should be aware that my teaching of the art, of which this book is a part, follows a directive imparted to me by Wen Shan Huang, the father of tai chi chuan in America. The problem, declared Huang, lay in the contradiction between the way tai chi chuan was traditionally taught in the "old country" (China), and our feeling and desire that tai chi chuan was the "grand jewel" that China should present to the American people.

This was in 1962 during the formation of the National Tai Chi Chuan Institute, which later became the National Tai Chi Chuan Association. The choice was between rigorous and secretive teaching to a few dozen "disciples" or to use popularized methods to reach thousands upon thousands of Americans who would derive some benefit from the famous "inner school" of martial art, even though it would be in a diluted, simplified way. The main thrust, it was decided, would be to popularize tai chi so it would become part of the public culture of the Western world.

Huang was in a unique position to make this decision. In China he had been a professor of economics at Nan King University, held a chair in Canton Province in culturology (a discipline composed of history, archeology, sociology, psychology, anthropology, and paleontology), and was a senator from Canton to the executive governing body. He also had a worldwide reputation. He was the translator of Joseph Needham's *Science and Society in China, Vol. 4,* and was considered the foremost totemic scholar in China. Peter Sirokin called Huang one of the top three sociologists in the world. He spoke a number of European languages, lectured at Columbia University, the New York School of Social Research, and many colleges and universities in California.

Therefore, he was monumentally qualified to combine Eastern and Western discipline to evaluate a human training of first magnitude, which is tai chi.

How could one question the authority of such a decision? My teacher Huang wanted to make tai chi accessible to a wide range of Western cultures, and I acquiesced to his directive that I spread tai chi "far and wide."

Thereupon, the National Tai Chi Chuan Association has always felt itself to be open to all groups, guided by Huang's vision which stressed international friendship, respect for ancient culture, and the philosophy behind the yin-yang. All these, he felt, should be taught in a manner anyone could understand.

As modern history began to unfold in the 60s on television and in print, and travelers from China began to proliferate, the world began to see pictures and reports of millions of Chinese on the streets at dawn doing tai chi chuan. Here, the policy of the National Tai Chi Chuan Association, under the guidance of Professor Huang and myself, was validated. In the 60s, Professor Huang and I had over 100 demonstrations and lectures on tai chi chuan.

In most cases, the therapeutic features of the discipline were emphasized. These included the subjects of centering, healing of many diseases, rejuvenation, longevity, moving meditation, and spiritual development. The Western world, especially America, began to see what is the jewel of the Chinese civilization.

Has it been a success? Yes. Where before there were but hundreds, there are now thousands in universities, YM and YWCAs, parks, etc., practicing the art. They have not been intimidated by the weightiness of the discipline, but have experienced the light, soft, rejuvenating qualities of the art.

Does that mean that the discipline as a respected martial art was negated? No, the contradiction has been resolved and in some areas there are quantitative to qualitative transformations and many senior students are delving deeper into the art and many are practicing tai chi martial art application.

Professor Huang's old age retired him from active teaching in the late 1970s and he died in his 90s a few years ago. At his behest, I took over the chairmanship of the National Tai Chi Chuan Association and carried on the policy and the progress of the group.   —M.H.

About the Author

Born in 1910, Marshall Ho'o began his involvement in martial arts the hard way—in the legendary alleys of San Francisco's Chinatown in the midst of the bloody Tong wars centered around Spofford Alley and Waverly Place.

In time, he became interested in Chinese martial arts, and began studying tai chi in 1946 with Choy Hok Pang. He also studied *el cuchillo* (Mexican knife fighting) in Guadalajara with a famous knife fighter at that time whose name was Santiago.

He became involved in commercial enterprises for a decade and worked until illness forced him to sell his business. He moved to Mexico seeking peace, quiet and recovery. There he practiced tai chi daily. His health improved as a result and in time he recovered completely.

The pen being the opposite of the sword, he predictably developed a thirst for scholarly pursuits as intense as his love for the martial arts. The quest for unity and wholeness led him to the study of theology, philosophy, history, science and medicine. For an intense period, Taoism, which is the philosophy

of tai chi chuan, became the vortex of inquiry.

The noted scholar Wen Shan Huang lived in Los Angeles and Ho'o sought him out and became his disciple. Huang was also a respected tai chi master of 40 years of practice and Ho'o became heir to his experience. Subsequently, Ho'o studied with Lo Sai Loan, Lo Sing, Tung Foo Ling, Mary Chow. *Sifu* (teacher) Howard Lee, an extraordinary instructor of Chinese kung fu, taught Ho'o the essentials of combat.

In turn, Ho'o taught tai chi at Cal Arts, UCLA, Cal State Northridge, Univeristy of Oriental Studies, Loyola-Marymont, and became founder and dean of the famous Aspen Academy of Martial Arts; and pioneered a nationwide TV tai chi program. More recently, Ho'o became chairman of the National Tai Chi Chuan Association. Then in recognition of his work, he was elected to the BLACK BELT magazine Hall of Fame.

At present he is a doctor of Oriental Medicine connected with the Center of Chinese Medicine and practicing acupuncture at the East-West Clinic. He has seven children ranging from ages 44 to four.

INTRODUCTION

What Is Tai Chi Chuan?

Tai chi chuan treats the individual body, mind, and spirit as a single phenomenon, so any proper definition is obliged to identify it as a single activity, but without omitting any of its many divergent applications. Tai chi chuan, also called tai chi, is self-defense on the most fundamental level, that of sustaining wholeness in every sense.

Tai chi is usually done slowly. This means that the practitioner becomes aware of every movement both large and small, and of the principles of movement. Moving slowly also accentuates the healthful benefits of the movements on the body; and the mind becomes thoroughly concentrated. Additionally, many insightful practitioners of tai chi are able to perceive its philosophical context, and that also becomes a quality invested in the movements so that the form and the content are one, and tai chi becomes art.

Physically, the wholeness of an individual can be assaulted by an enemy or by illness. Tai chi movements, in this respect, can be applied to self-defense. They also promote health by improving the flow of *chi* (life energy) from the lower psychic center, a locus three inches below the navel called the *tan tien,* and throughout the entire body. In addition these movements calm the mind and thus benefit mental health as well.

As a form of activity, tai chi can be described as ritualistic. Its meaning however, is not buried far away in China, but rather is to be found in the archetypal attributes of every person, and in the unfolding of the existential condition. This other side can be fully grasped when tai chi is practiced regularly. When practiced regularly and ritualistically, it helps fortify the wholeness of one's humanity and keeps it from being fragmented. One is able to feel the interplay of the original primal opposites which are the source of our polarized psychic state, and which in Chinese cosmology are called *yin* and *yang*.

This polarity, down through the centuries, has been observed by wisemen in the esoteric traditions of both East and West. Because of it, we have consciousness, the double-edged sword with which we create or destroy. Tai chi attempts to bring about a more effective dialectic, promoting creativity as well as peace in the soul. The tai chi symbol represents this idea.

Consciousness sets us free, but it also cuts us off from that state of unquestioning participation in nature which is full of meaning. And so, we find ourselves situated at the threshold of a great void, which is our new home. The way of transforming this void into a place where human life can remain whole and integrated is called, in the Chinese tradition, the Tao. Tai chi, at its highest order, apprehends the mystery of the Tao.

How Is Tai Chi Learned?

The first step in learning tai chi is studying the movements of the form. This provides the practitioner with a structure within which the other five steps take place.

The second step is training in the correct way of performing the formal movements which is with circularity, stressing flow and coordination.

Third is the training of intrinsic energy, the result of using the body as one whole unit to exert force.

Training in directing the flow of chi throughout the body is the fourth step.

The fifth step is training the spirit. This is the meditative aspect of tai chi.

The sixth and final step is the coordination of internal and external movements.

Using these six steps, the practitioner tries to accomplish certain goals. In order: he trains his body to generate more intrinsic energy; he controls this energy with consciousness; he brings his body, mind, and spirit into harmony; he transforms his spirit into the void; he transforms the void into the Tao.

Why Practice Tai Chi?

Regular tai chi practice enchances the function of the central nervous system, keeps the joints flexible, the muscles toned, and improves the operation of internal organs. The slow, soft movements tend to neutralize the stress and tension resultant of modern urban culture. The Chinese people, in spite of low economic circumstances, are a visibly healthy race. It is worth noting that a quarter of a billion people (more than the total population of the United States) daily practice tai chi in China.

Done correctly, tai chi invigorates the human organism by stimulating the chi which courses through conduits of the body known in acupuncture as meridians. Fourteen major meridians network the entire body. At specific locations, known as points on the meridian lines, the organs of the body can be stimulated. This stimulation can be affected by invasive techniques such as acupuncture or moxibustion, or as in tai chi, by movements concentrated or focused on the area. The desired result is a balancing of the polarized forces of yin and yang, and this induces and maintains well being.

Tai chi, moving all areas of the human body, thus activates the meridian network to reduce congestion and strengthen weak functions. Refinement of this knowledge through centuries created a concommittance of martial art and therapeutic techniques which resulted in the reputation of tai chi as the finest exercise for human health.

Who, Where, and When?

Chang-San Feng, a hermit alchemist living at Mol-Don mountain in China 800 years ago, first received the techniques of tai chi chuan in a dream, according to legend. It is said that Feng was searching for the elixer of life. Because it is legend, this story seems truer to the nature of tai chi chuan than other, more realistic accounts which say it evolved from previously existing styles of boxing.

In the late 18th century, Wang Tsung-yueh formalized the art and provided its philosophical context drawn from Taoism. Then, in 1852, Yang Lu Chan brought tai chi from Honan Province to Beijing. From Beijing, it spread throughout China, and branched out into many different styles—the most widespread today is the Yang style.

Words can only take you so far toward an understanding of tai chi. Although lowering the microscope of language on the subject brings it into focus, eventually there comes a point at which approaching closer puts it out of focus again. For further insight, a new instrument is required. You must begin practice.

Contents

NINE TEMPLE EXERCISES

Asian monks and nuns are usually very healthy. A simple diet, tranquil sur-roundings, constant prayers and meditations contribute much to their well-being. Most important, physical movements known as temple exercises are practiced to offset the possibility of physical flabbiness or atrophy which could be a result of their gentle environment.

Usually the routine is comprised of ten or less forms. The performing pace is slow and without tension, minimizing fatigue residuals. The *chi* (internal energy) meridians are stimulated and the set of varied movements adequately tunes the body.

However, used as an exercising system by itself, the form repetitions are multiplied, usually from ten to 30 or so. Done morning and again at night, the benefits are notable.

TEMPLE EXERCISE: ONE

The first exercise is known as the prayer wheel. In this one exercise, the whole body is toned. It invigorates the four systems: the vascular, the lymphatic, the nervous, and the chi systems.

PRAYER WHEEL

(1) Point your left toe out at a 45-degree angle. Put your weight on it and lift your right foot up gently, and step forward, placing your heel first and then your toes pointing forward. Make sure there's a transverse distance between your feet of four to six inches. (2) Raise both hands, palms facing each other, up to shoulder height and about one foot apart. (3) Rock back on your left leg and pull your hands in toward you in a circular path. (4) As your hands come in toward you, circle them down and begin shifting your weight to your forward leg. (5) When your hands circle completely outward, your weight is shifted so your forward knee is just over your toes. Your knee must never extend beyond your toes, then (6) begin another circle as you rock back on your left leg once again. As you rock back and forth, do not increase or decrease your height, but keep your body on the same level throughout.

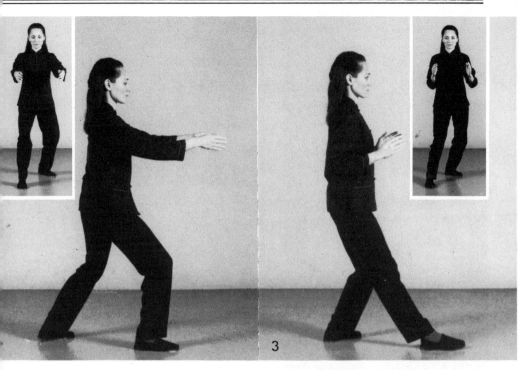

3

6

1

3

TEMPLE EXERCISE: TWO
The knee is the site of six major acupuncture points. If you do this exercise you can prevent arthritis in your middle and old age.

KNEE ROTATION

(1) With feet together, flex your knees, and bend forward at the hips to incline your torso, placing your hands on your knees face forward and keep your back straight though it is inclined. This position should be maintained from the center of the body, not by supporting your weight with your hands. Think of it this way: the hands aren't really there. (2) Rotate the knees together, circling over to the left, then (3) back, to the (4) right, and (5) forward once again. Repeat a series of rotations to the right, and then an equal number to the left.

2

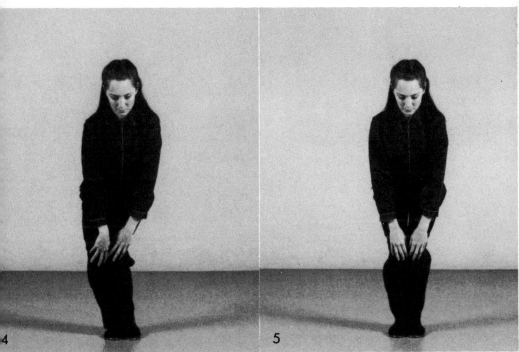

4

5

The crossed arm rotation posture is a challenge stance from which you strike alternately with one hand and then the other. This exercise activates the spleen and the kidneys.

CROSSED ARM ROTATION

(1) Stand with feet squared, toes forward, shoulder width apart. Flex your knees slightly, and extend your arms out to either side at shoulder level. (2) Keeping your feet planted, and minimizing the movement of your hips, swing your right arm over to slap your left palm. Most of the twisting of your body takes place from the waist up. (3&4) Swing your right hand back to its original position as your head faces forward. (5) Next, swing your left hand over to the right side to slap your right palm, your head turns 90 degrees to the right, then (6&7) return your left hand back to its original position as your head faces forward.

1

4

5

3

7

1

TEMPLE EXERCISE: FOUR

In this exercise imagine that you're picking fruit from a tree. This is one of the oldest movements in mankind. We have done this throughout a million years of history. It is a survival practice—searching for food, reaching for something to eat. This exercise activates the kidneys, the spleen, and the pancreas. These organs are all activated and the joints are lifted. This is a very important movement. Simple, very simple to do, but very, very complex insofar as the meridians are concerned.

3

PICKING FRUIT

(1) With feet only slightly spread, toes forward, reach with both hands overhead. (2) Stretch upward with the right arm, then (3) return to the starting position, and (4) stretch upward with the left arm. Keep alternating right and left.

1

3

TEMPLE EXERCISE: FIVE

This exercise helps eliminate indigestion and constipation, and most important of all, it invigorates the reproductive system. It requires a little warm-up in order to swing the leg way up and so is placed on the latter half of the list of the nine exercises. Remember this is a leg swing, not a kick.

LEG SWING

(1) Put your two feet together with the left foot at a 45-degree angle. (2) With your right knee slightly flexed, swing your right leg forward, (3) back through the middle like a pendulum and (4) back behind you. Keep your upper body relaxed.

1

3

TEMPLE EXERCISE: SIX

This exercise invigorates the spine, up and down. Invigoration of the spine is very important to your health. Many healing arts are based upon the well-being of the spine, chiropractics, for example. Energy goes all the way up to the post-pituitary and the cortex to affect even the thinking process. Do this movement for about five minutes and you will feel quite thoroughly invigorated.

LEG BOUNCE

(1) Put your body weight on your left leg and extend your right foot out about a foot, placing the toes on the ground with the heel raised about a half inch. Flex your left knee. You are now on the thigh muscle of the left leg. Keep your back straight as you (2) lower yourself about four inches and (3) come back up to your original position. (4) Repeat in a pulsating rhythm and then exchange legs. Your entire weight is on the heel of the foot so that there's a line of projection right from the spine all the way up to the top of the skull. Relax the arms, relax the body, and move the energy straight up as though you're cleaning a chimney flue. The chi flows all up and down from the top of the head all the way down to the heel.

TEMPLE EXERCISE: SEVEN

This is what we have to do in life all the time—retreat and advance. The kidneys, the liver, the spleen, the pancreas, gall bladder, ascending colon, transverse, and descending colon are all set in motion.

RETREAT AND ADVANCE

(1) Start with your feet about 18 inches apart. (2) Turn your body to face to the right, keeping your feet planted, then (3) shift your body back away from the direction you're facing. (4&5) With your weight still on your left leg turn to face in the other direction, and then (6) retreat once again. You may retreat only about a foot, but it's a distinct retreat. The whole body stays loose. Only the legs are in action. In retreating imagine a force coming toward you from which you retreat, (7) stopping when your ear, shoulder, hip, knee, and toes are in a straight line. That's as far as you can go without toppling over. Now, in life you don't always retreat.

1

4

5

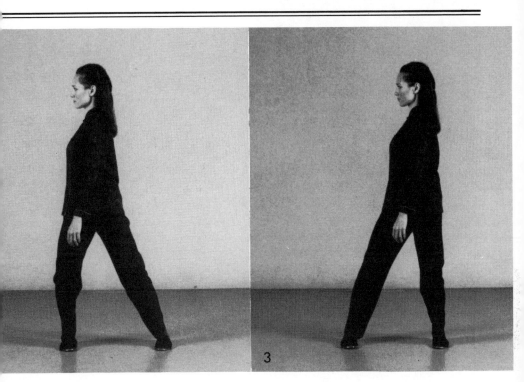

3

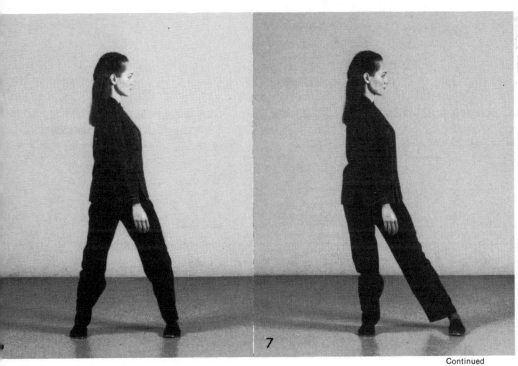

7

Continued

You also have to advance. (8) Face forward. (9) Turn to face left. (10) Move your body toward the direction you face, stopping when all your weight is shifted to your left leg and again ear, shoulder, hip, knee, and toes are in a line. (11&12) Turn to face in the other direction, and (13&14) advance in the same manner. Keep your posture erect.

8

11

12

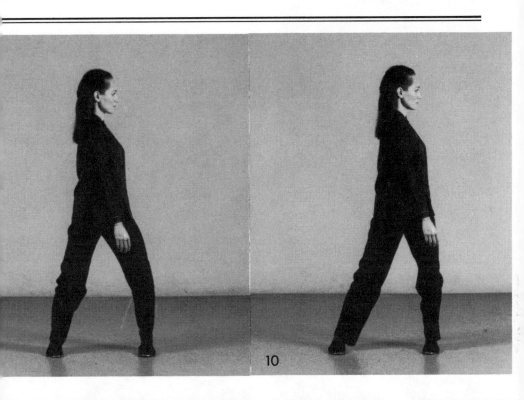

10

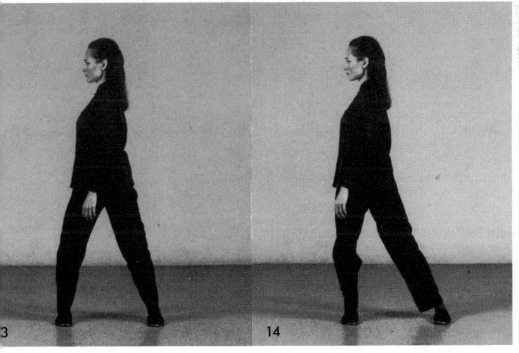

3

14

TEMPLE EXERCISE: EIGHT

In this exercise imagine there's a stone table in front of you which comes up to the height of your knees. The stone table is the place where you will grind cereal. Imagine further that you are holding two bricks, one in each hand, and with them you are grinding corn on the table.

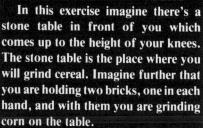

GRINDING CORN

(1) Put your feet about two feet apart. Both feet are parallel, and staunchly firm upon the ground. Your knees are bent, your hands are dropped, and your back is inclined but straight. Your thighs take most of your body weight. (2) Move your hands in two separate intersecting circles. (3&4) Circle to the right, with your right hand, (5) come back through center to complete the right circle, and then (6-8) circle to the left with the left hand. (9) Come back through the center to complete the circle, and then repeat. The fatigue entailed in this type of movement is lessened by the rhythm of the movement.

1

TEMPLE EXERCISE: NINE

With this exercise we come back to civilization, back to urban society where we have mirrors. This exercise has a tremendous effect on the lower back, on the backs of the knees, which are rarely exercised, and on the inside of the thighs. Many martial arts work the exterior muscles, but do not exercise the interior muscles of the thighs. This exercise is good for the kidneys; and an area that's not mentioned very much—do this and you won't get hemorrhoids.

POLISHING THE MIRROR

(1) Keep your feet about a foot or a foot and a half apart. Imagine you are holding two rags in front of a large round mirror. Begin with your hands side by side at a height just above your head. (2) Begin to separate your hands, (3) circling the left out to the left side and the right out to the right side. (4-6) As you come down the outside of this imaginary round mirror, your hands, following its outline come together in the center as you

4

3

6

Continued

7

(7) come to a full squatting position, Keep your back straight and your palms vertical. (8-12) Stand up, keeping your hands side by side as you go up to your original starting position to begin again. Remember to keep moving on the same plane at all times and not allow any part of your body to touch or pass through that plane.

10

9

11

12

EIGHT-MINUTE FORM

There is no exact history of archaic tai chi chuan. The more recent centuries founded five main schools following the same principles and general teachings and techniques. However, each group features distinct variations in postures and applications.

All movements are lyrical, graceful, natural, soft and purposeful, but within they are firm—like an iron hand in a velvet glove.

The usual 108 movements in the classical long form necessitates 35 minutes to complete. The People's Republic of China, in the early days of their modernization, convened many masters to create a shorter set of forms, approximately 30.

The instructions contained herein, called the eight-minute form, follows that trend. Though simplified, this short form retains the basic features and benefits of the long traditional system. Therefore, regular practice of this short form will likewise improve and maintain physical well-being.

While practicing tai chi, intense concentration is necessary. Breathing should be deep, even, tranquil, and coordinated with the movements.

COMMENCEMENT OF TAI CHI

(1) Stand with your feet shoulder width apart, your weight distributed evenly on both feet, toes pointing forward. Relax your arms at your sides. Keep your chin drawn slightly inward. Do not protrude your chest or draw in your stomach. (2) Bring your arms up slowly to shoulder level, keeping your elbows and shoulders down and relaxed. Your hands should be relaxed so there's a slight curve in your fingers. (3&4) Flex your knees as you simultaneously press your palms down gently, lowering your arms. Keep your waist relaxed and your buttocks slightly pulled in. *IMPORTANT POINTS:* The body should remain quiescient throughout. The spirit should be concentrated, with emphasis on "emptiness." Chi should be lowered to the *tan tien* (the psychic center located three inches below the navel). Deeper meanings can gradually be comprehended from the spiritual, psychological, and physical points of view.

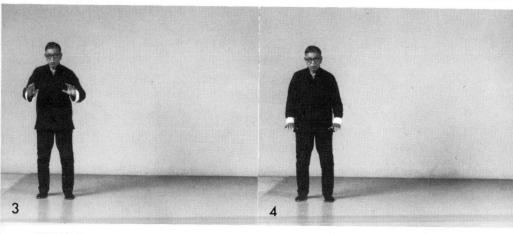

3

4

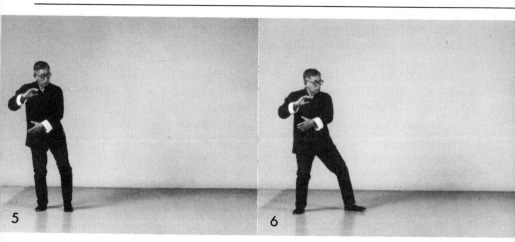

5

6

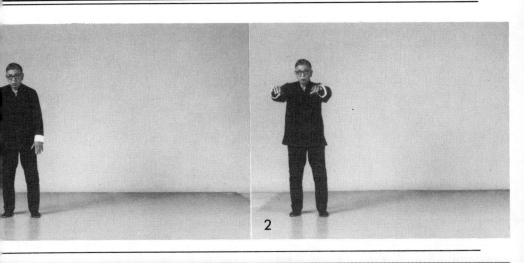

2

PARTING THE WILD HORSE'S MANE

(5&6) As you shift your weight to your right foot, turn your torso slightly to the right. At the same time your right hand comes up to chest level palm down, and your left hand swings under to waist level palm up. Your two hands should be positioned as if holding a large ball between them. This is called the *hold ball* gesture. (7) Turn your body to the left as you step out to the left with your left foot, placing your heel first and then your entire foot. As you turn, (8) raise your left hand and extend it forward with elbow slightly bent, palm facing obliquely upward, and lower your right hand to the right side palm down, fingers forward. Shift your weight to your left leg so that your right leg straightens but does not lock, and your right toes angle out at 45 degrees while your left toes point straight ahead. Do not let your left knee go beyond your toes. This is called

8

Continued

the *bow stance*. (9) Shift your weight to your right leg as if sitting back. Your left leg straightens as a result and your left toes are raised off the floor. Pivot your left toes outward at a 45-degree angle. As you shift your weight forward again, place your entire left foot on the floor and bring your left hand back to the left side of your chest, palm down while you bring your right hand in front of your left hip palm up for a hold ball gesture. (10) Step forward with your right foot, placing the heel first and then the toes pointing straight ahead. (11) As you shift your weight to your right foot, extend your right hand as you lower your left hand to the left side of your waist palm down, fingers forward, establishing (12) a right bow stance. (13)

9

12

Sit back, raising the toes of your right foot, pointing them outward at a 45-degree angle, and shift your weight forward again as you bring your right hand to your chest and your left hand across to the right side of your abdomen for (14&15) hold ball gesture. Step forward with your left foot, placing the heel first, and (16) shift your weight onto your left foot placing the toes pointing straight ahead as you raise your left hand from your waist and extend it up and forward, and bring your right hand palm down to the right side, fingers pointing forward for another left bow stance. *IMPORTANT POINTS:* Maintain a circular form with your arms. Use your waist as the axis when turning.

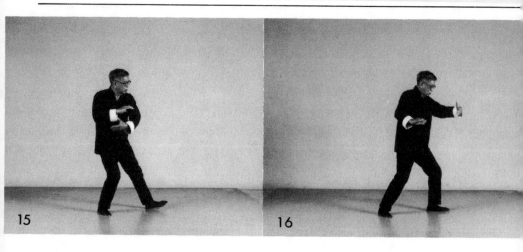

15

16

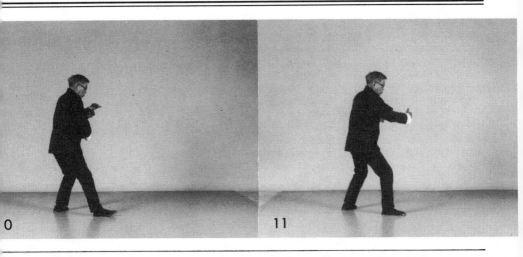

0

11

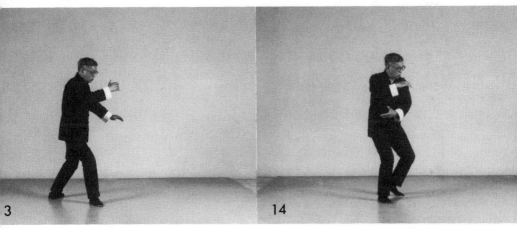

3

14

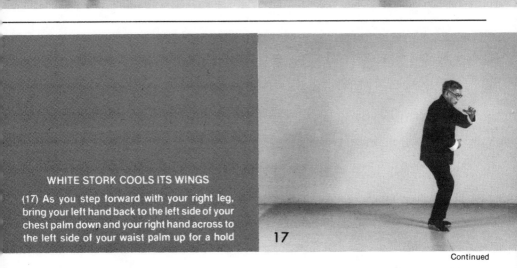

WHITE STORK COOLS ITS WINGS

(17) As you step forward with your right leg, bring your left hand back to the left side of your chest palm down and your right hand across to the left side of your waist palm up for a hold

17

Continued

ball gesture. (18) Place your heel first as you step with your right foot turning your toes out at a 45-degree angle. (19) Shifting your weight to your right foot, place your entire right foot on the floor, and begin raising your right hand upward and to the right side as you lower your left hand to the left side. (20) Step forward with your left foot, keeping your weight on your right. Place your left foot down with the heel raised off the floor for an *empty stance* as you extend your right hand up and to the right and lower your left to the left side. *IMPORTANT POINTS:* The torso is lowered, sitting on the right leg. The chest should not be thrust forward. Your two arms should maintain a semi-circle.

18

BRUSH KNEE

(21) Turn your torso slightly to the left as your right hand moves down and your left hand moves up. Raise your left foot and (22) step forward, placing your heel first. Your right hand circles downward past your torso and then upward behind your right ear while your left hand comes back toward your chest. (23&24) As you shift your weight forward to your left foot, placing your entire foot on the floor, press forward with your hand, palm forward, and lower your right hand to waist level as you circle it palm down forward over your left knee, and over to

21

24

the left side. (25&26) Sit back, shifting your weight to your right leg as you raise your left toes and point them outward 45 degrees. Shift your weight forward to your left leg, turning your torso slightly to the left as you down and back, and bring your right hand toward your

9   20

2   23

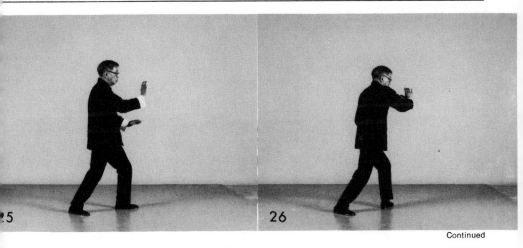

.5   26

Continued

chest. (27) Step forward with your right leg as you circle your left hand up behind your left ear and press forward with it palm forward. Meanwhile, bring your lower hand from chest level to waist level and circle it forward over your right

27

29

PLAYING THE HARP

(30) Step forward half a step with your right foot. (31) Shift your weight back on your right leg as you extend your left hand upward and to the front, simultaneously withdrawing your right hand downward and back to a position inside your left elbow. *IMPORTANT POINTS:* Lower the shoulders, bend the elbows, and relax the chest. The movement of raising the right hand should describe an arc, and should be done without jerking. In moving the hands outward, the strength of the spinal column should be applied.

REPULSE THE MONKEY

(32) Circle your right hand down and back past your torso. (33) As you bring it up and press it palm forward past your right ear, step back with your left foot, placing toes first and then the heel, and turn your left hand palm up. (34&35) Shift your weight back on your left leg as you press forward with your right palm and withdraw your left hand palm up, circling it

32

knee and out to the right side. (28) Sit back on your left leg, raising your right toes and turning them outward 45 degrees. Shift your weight forward to your right leg as you circle your right hand down and back while drawing your left back toward your chest. (29) Step forward with your left foot as you circle your right hand up behind your right ear and press forward with it palm forward. Meanwhile, lower your right hand from chest level to waist level palm down and circle it forward over your left knee and out to the left side. *IMPORTANT POINTS:* Do not use the limbs to turn the waist and thighs, but instead use the waist as the axis of pivot for movement of the limbs.

28

0

31

3

34

Continued

down and back. (36) Step back with your right foot as you circle your left hand up and press it palm forward past your left ear. (37) As your left palm comes forward, withdraw your right hand palm up, (38) circling it downward and back as

35

you shift your weight to your right leg. (39) Step back with your left foot as you circle your right hand up and press it palm forward past your right ear. (40) As your right palm comes forward, withdraw your left hand palm up. (41) circling it downward and back as you shift your

38

weight to your left leg. (42) Step back with your right foot as you circle your left hand up and press it palm forward past your left ear. (43) As your left palm comes forward, withdraw your right hand palm up, circling it down and back as you shift your weight to your right leg. *IMPORTANT POINTS:* When the center of gravity is shifted to the right leg, the left turns into an insubstantial step, and vice versa. Movements in this form are of an uneven number. The transverse distance between your two feet is shoulder width. The retreating feet proceed in straight lines.

41

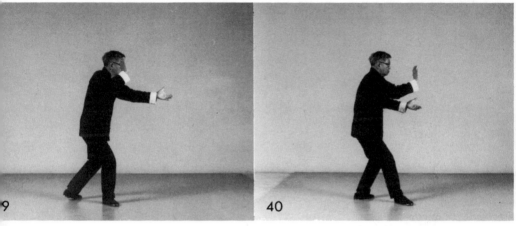

Continued

GRASP THE BIRD'S TAIL — LEFT

(44) Circle your right hand up and over to a palm down position in front of the right side of your chest. At the same time, swing your left hand down and under to a palm up position below your right hand for a hold ball gesture, bringing your left leg in toward your right. (45) Step forward with your left foot, placing the heel first and then the toes, and shift your weight forward to your left leg into a left bow stance. At the same time extend your left hand forward palm inward as if fending off a blow with your right hand following six inches behind it palm down in a horizontal position. (46) From the bow stance, turn your left hand palm up and drop it under your right hand. When both palms

44

face each other, begin to shift your weight back, pivoting your torso to the right. Begin to circle your right hand down and back as you turn it palm up, and turn your left palm facing to the right as if pulling with both hands. (47) Continue circling your right hand. As it comes back past your torso, shift your weight back on your right leg and withdraw your left hand to your chest. (48) As your right hand comes over your right shoulder, press it palm forward at shoulder height. Extend your left hand palm inward. Your right palm presses forward about four inches behind your left wrist which also moves forward. (49) Pass your right palm over your left wrist as you turn your left palm downward. Sway your right hand out to the

47

right and your left hand out to the left so they become parallel to one another, palms down at eye level with arms extended. (50) Draw both hands back toward your torso along a curve as you shift your weight back on your right leg, and then press them both palms forward as you shift your weight forward once again. *IM-PORTANT POINTS:* The focus is on the waist, which is always considered the axis of a wheel. Breathing should be natural, keeping the mouth closed, but not tightly, with the tip of the tongue touching the upper palate. The shoulders are lowered and a bow-shape is maintained with the two arms in front of the torso.

50

45

46

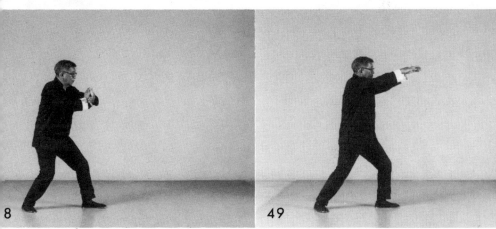

48

49

GRASP THE BIRD'S TAIL — RIGHT

(51) Turn to the right by shifting your weight on your right leg, pivoting your left foot on the heel to turn the toes to the right, and turning your torso to the right. As you shift your weight back on your left leg, swing your right hand under to a palm up position and your right hand over to

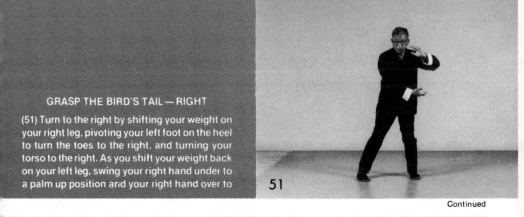

51

Continued

a palm up position for a hold ball gesture. (52) Bring your right leg in toward your left and step out to the right with your right foot, placing the heel first and then the toes, shift your weight to your right leg for a right bow stance. At the same time extend your right hand forward palm inward as if fending off a blow with your left hand following six inches behind it palm down in a horizontal position. (53) From the bow stance, turn your right hand palm up and drop it down under your left hand. When both palms face each other, begin to shift your weight back, pivoting your torso to the left. Begin to circle your left hand down and back as you turn it palm up, and turn your right palm facing to the left as if pulling with both hands.

52

54

55

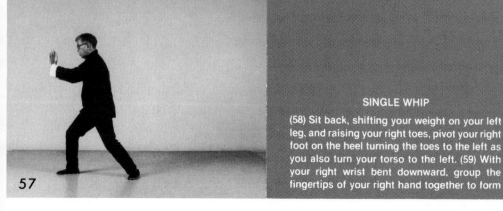

57

SINGLE WHIP

(58) Sit back, shifting your weight on your left leg, and raising your right toes, pivot your right foot on the heel turning the toes to the left as you also turn your torso to the left. (59) With your right wrist bent downward, group the fingertips of your right hand together to form

(54) Continue circling your left hand. As it comes past your torso, shift your weight back on your left leg and withdraw your right hand to your chest. (55) As your left hand comes over your left shoulder, press it palm forward at shoulder height. Extend your right hand palm inward. Your left palm presses forward about four inches behind your right wrist which also moves forward. Pass your left palm over right wrist as you turn your right palm downward. Sway your left hand out to the left side and your right hand out to the right so they become parallel to one another, palms down at eye level with arms extended. (56) Draw both hands back toward your torso along a curve as you shift your weight back on your left leg, and

3

then (57) press them both palms forward as you shift your weight forward once again. *IM-PORTANT POINTS:* The focus is on the waist, which is always considered the axis of a wheel. Breathing should be natural, keeping the mouth closed, but not tightly, with the tip of the tongue touching the upper palate. The shoulders are lowered and a bow-shape is maintained with the two arms in front of the torso.

6

58

59

Continued

an eagle's beak, and (60) circle it inward toward your chest. (61) Shift your weight to your right leg and extend your eagle's beak out obliquely to the right. (62) Step out with your left foot, placing the heel first as you extend your left hand out to the left. (63) Shift your weight to your left leg, placing your entire left foot down to establish a left bow stance. *IMPORTANT POINTS:* Keep the upper body erect. Relax the waist. Avoid leaning forward. While the right elbow is slightly bent, the left elbow and left knee form a vertical line. In transitional movements, the upper and lower parts of the body are synchronized.

60

63

WAVE HANDS LIKE CLOUDS

(64) Sit back on your right leg, lifting your left toes. Pivot your left foot on the heel, turning the toes to the left as you also turn your torso to the left. (65) When you wave your hands, your right hand waves in a clockwise circle and your left hand in a counterclockwise circle. Begin with your right hand by circling it from the top to the bottom of its circle as you shift

your weight to your right leg. (66) As your right hand comes up in front of you, your left hand goes down. (67) Step in with your right foot bringing your feet together as your right hand comes to the top and your left hand reaches bottom. (68) As your left hand comes up in front of you, and your right hand goes down, shift

66

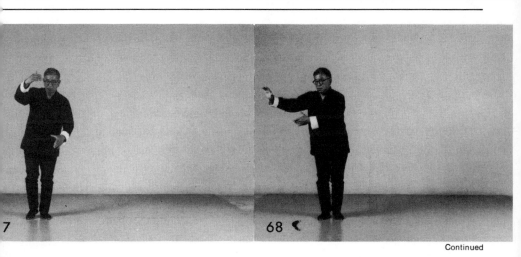

61

62

64

65

67

68 ◄

Continued

your weight to your right leg. (69&70) Step to the left with your left foot as your left hand reaches top and your right hand reaches bottom. (71) As your right hand comes up in front of you and your left hand goes down, shift your weight to your left leg. (72) Step in with your right foot, bringing your feet together as your right hand comes to the top and your left hand reaches bottom. (73) As your left hand comes up in front of you and your right hand goes down, shift your weight to your right leg. (74&75) Step to the left with your left foot as your left hand reaches top and your right

69

72

73

reaches bottom. (76) As your right hand comes up in front of you and your left hand goes down, shift your weight to your left leg. (77) Step to the right with your right foot as your right hand reaches top and your left hand reaches bottom. (78) Shift your weight to your right leg and step in with your left as your right hand goes down to bottom and your left hand

76

0

71

4

75

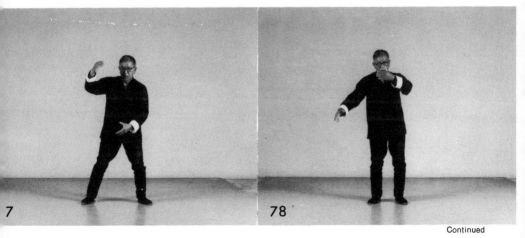

7

78

Continued

comes up to the top. (79) Shift your weight to your right leg as your right hand comes up in front of you and your left hand goes down. (80) Step to the right with your right foot as your right hand comes to the top and your left hand reaches bottom. (81) Step in with your left foot as your right hand circles to the bottom and

79

your left hand circles to the top. (82) Shift your weight to your left leg and step out with your right as your right hand comes up and your left goes down. *IMPORTANT POINTS:* This is one of the most important forms in tai chi. Avoid jerking up and down while pivoting the torso at the waist. Movements of the knees should follow movements of the left or right hand, whether the direction is up or down. The arms, elbows, hands, legs, and knees are considered as wheels. In operation they seem to be extending and yet not extending, contracting and not contracting.

82

84

85

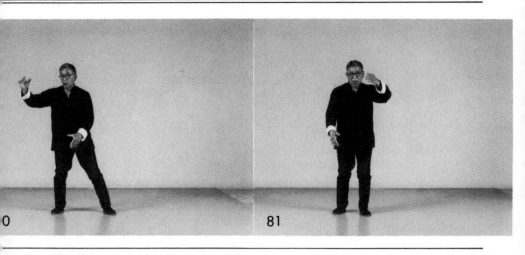

0

81

SINGLE WHIP

(83) Shift your weight to your right leg as you continue to circle your left hand upward. to chest level. Form your right hand into an eagle's beak and extend it obliquely out to the right side. (84) Continue to circle your left hand upward. Sit back on your right leg and pivot your left foot to point to the side as you turn your body in that direction. (85) Arc your left hand over as you shift your weight forward into a left bow stance. *IMPORTANT POINTS:* Keep the upper body erect. Relax the waist. Avoid leaning forward. While the right elbow is slightly bent, the left elbow and left knee form a vertical line. In transitional movements. the upper and lower parts of the body are synchronized.

83

HIGH PAT ON HORSE

(86) Place your right foot half a step forward and sit back on your right leg, raising your left heel to establish a left empty stance. Mean-

86

Continued

while, open your right hand. (87) Press your right hand palm forward at shoulder level as you withdraw your left hand. *IMPORTANT POINTS:* Do not raise the chest or bow the back. Keep the right hand at eyebrow level. Strength is concentrated on the right palm as it moves forward. Coordinate the rising and dropping of the legs with the raising and lowering of the hands.

87

and your right hand to the right. (89&90) Step down with your left foot, into a left bow stance, toes turned out 45 degrees, as you circle both hands out to the sides, downward and then up in front of your torso. As they overlap in front of you palms inward, your left hand is on the inside. (91) Turn them palms out as you separate them, shifting your weight forward to your left

89

leg. (92) Sweep both hands out to the sides as you raise your knee and then extend your right foot out and up to just above waist level. *IMPORTANT POINTS:* Do not bend forward or look upward. During the separation of the two hands, the wrists are at shoulder height. The movement of the hands should be harmonious with stepping.

92

KICK WITH RIGHT FOOT

(88) Bring your left hand up, palm up, to cross over your right wrist. Raise your left foot as you separate your hands by turning them palms foward, and sweeping your left hand to the left

88

91

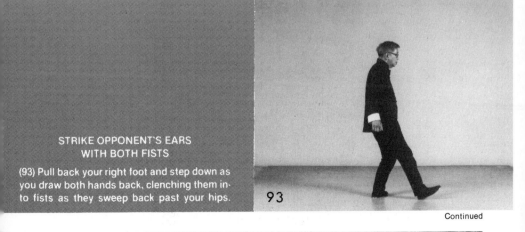

STRIKE OPPONENT'S EARS
WITH BOTH FISTS

(93) Pull back your right foot and step down as you draw both hands back, clenching them into fists as they sweep back past your hips.

93

Continued

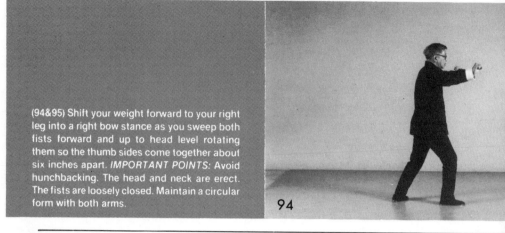

(94&95) Shift your weight forward to your right leg into a right bow stance as you sweep both fists forward and up to head level rotating them so the thumb sides come together about six inches apart. *IMPORTANT POINTS:* Avoid hunchbacking. The head and neck are erect. The fists are loosely closed. Maintain a circular form with both arms.

94

96

97

99

100

TURN AND KICK WITH LEFT SOLE

(96) Sit back on your left leg and pivot your right foot to point to the left as you turn your torso to the left. At the same time open your hands palm outward and spread them out to either side of your body in wide circles. (97) Shift your weight to your right leg as both hands circle downward. (98) As both hands come upward in front of you, palms in with your right crossing inside your left, bring your left foot in toward your

right. (99&100) Lifting your knee first, kick with your left sole as you turn your hands palms out and swing them out to the sides. *IMPORTANT POINTS:* Coordinate the separation of the hands with kicking with the sole. Your torso should be erect without a forward slant. During the kick, lower the torso.

SNAKE CREEPS DOWN LEFT SIDE

(101) Pull back your left foot and step down, forming your right hand into an eagle's beak.

101

Continued

(102) Squat down on your right leg, circling your left hand back to sweep down past the front of your left shoulder, down the left side of your torso, and across the inside of your extended left leg. Meanwhile, bring your right hand down and in toward the front of your body. (103) As you shift your weight forward and come back up, sweep the left hand palm down in a horizontal curve forward over the left knee and out to the left side while continuing to bring your right hand under across the front of your body. *IMPORTANT POINTS:* Coordinate the movement of the arms and knees with lowering and raising the torso. Keep the spine straight throughout the movement. As the right hand comes to the back of the torso, it makes a semi-circle. The left hand moving downward and forward makes a semi-circle.

GOLDEN COCKEREL STANDS ON LEFT LEG

(104) As you stand up, your left hand circles out to the left side palm down and your right continues to come forward across your body and up. (105) Shift your weight entirely on your left leg as you bring your right leg forward. (106&107) Open your right hand as it comes up to eye level and bring your right knee forward and up. *IMPORTANT POINTS:* The leg bearing the full weight is bent slightly. The torso is erect, emphasizing balance and stability.

104

107

SNAKE CREEPS DOWN RIGHT LEG

(108) Form your left hand into an eagle's beak. Bring your right foot back behind you as you step down. Sweep your right hand down in front of your left shoulder. Shift your weight back on your right leg and pivot your left foot on the heel (109) to point to the right. At the same time, turn your body to the right as you sweep your right hand down and to the right.

02

103

05

106

08

109

Continued

(110&111) Squat down on your left leg as you sweep your right hand across your body and down along the inside of your extended right leg. Bring your left hand forward across the front of your body. *IMPORTANT POINTS:* Coordinate the movement of the arms and knees with lowering and raising the torso. Keep the spine straight throughout the movement. As the right hand comes to the back of the torso, it makes a semi-circle. The left hand moving downward and forward makes a semi-circle.

110

112

113

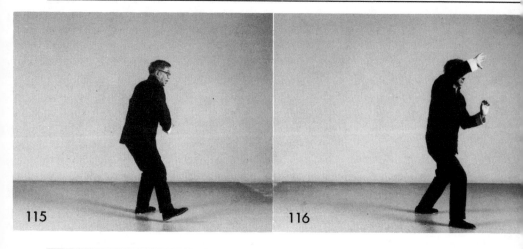

115

116

1

GOLDEN COCKEREL STANDS ON RIGHT LEG

(112) Shift your weight forward to your right leg and bring your left leg forward. At the same time, continue to bring your left hand forward. (113) Raise your left knee as your left hand comes forward and up. Your right hand circles over your right knee and out to the right side palm down. *IMPORTANT POINTS:* The leg bearing the full weight is bent slightly. The torso is erect, emphasizing balance and stability.

WORK AT SHUTTLES ON BOTH SIDES

(114) Step back with your left foot. (115) Shift your weight on your left leg as you pivot your right toes to point out 45 degrees to the right, and perform a hold ball gesture with your left hand on top palm down and your right hand on the bottom palm up. (116) Shift your weight for a right bow stance to your right leg. At the same time bring your right hand above your head on the right side, palm inclined upward, and push your left hand palm forward at chest

114

level. (117) Shift your weight entirely on your right leg as you bring your left foot in to your right as you form a hold ball gesture with your right hand on top palm down and your left hand on the bottom palm up. Step forward with

117

Continued

your left foot 45 degrees to the left, and (118) as you shift your weight forward on your left leg for a left bow stance, bring your left hand above your head on the left side, and press your right hand palm forward at chest level. *IMPORTANT POINTS:* Avoid raising the shoulders. There are differences between revolving the torso and turning it.

118

lowered. (120) Then pull up your left foot and place it down on the toes for a left empty stance and drop your right hand diagonally downward from the upper right side to a low position directly in front of your body. Your left hand is also lowered. (121&122) As you turn your body back toward the right, bring your right hand above your head on the right side, palm inclined upward, and press your left hand palm forward at chest level. At the same time, step forward with your left foot into a left bow stance. *IMPORTANT POINTS:* In bringing the right hand down, do not lean the shoulders forward. The center of gravity is on the right leg, but may shift to the left leg.

120

FAN THROUGH BACK

(123) Shift your weight back on your right leg, and pivot your left foot by the heel to point your toes to the right as you also turn your body to the right. Both hands sweep over to the right as well. (124) Continue to circle your left hand out to the right side and downward as you (125) shift your weight to your left leg. Continue to circle your right hand down and under, and as it crosses in front of your abdomen, clench it into a fist with knuckles up. *IMPORTANT POINTS:* The strength of the spinal cord can reach the two hands. Stretch the back muscles, lower the shoulders, left hand level with the nose.

123

NEEDLE AT SEA BOTTOM

(119) Bring your right foot toward your left a half a step and swing your right arm to the right, first curving it down and then back up in the shape of a U, while your right hand is

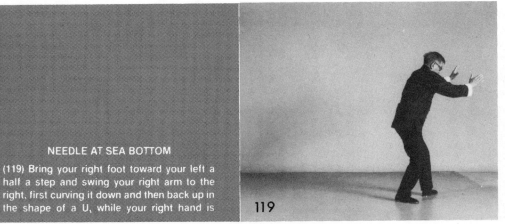

119

21

122

24

125

Continued

TURN AND CHOP WITH FIST

(126) Pull your right foot toward your left and step out with your right foot to the right as you continue to circle your right fist upward in front of your body and out to the right. Meanwhile, your left hand circles downward and in toward the front of your body. (127) As your right fist circles down on the right side, knuckles down, your left hand crosses your body and comes up on the right side adjacent to your right fist.

126

128

129

131

132

27

(128&129) Swing your right fist in a figure-eight pattern, first, diagonally downward to the right and then upward on he right as you shift your weight back on your left leg. (130) Your right fist then comes diagonally downward across the front of your body. Your left hand swings down and back. At the same time, begin to bring your

30

right foot in toward your left foot. (131) As your right fist circles upward in front of your body, your left hand comes upward behind you. At the same time, step forward with your right foot, turning your toes out 45 degrees to the right. (132) As you swing your right fist over and down, knuckles down, bring your left hand over and forward adjacent to your right fist, and shift your weight forward to your right leg. *IMPORTANT POINTS:* Movement of the arms and legs is accomplished by turning the waist and spine.

STEP, PARRY, PUNCH

(133) Step forward with your left foot as your right fist prepares to push from your right side.

133

Continued

(134&135) Punch forward slowly with your right fist, thumb side up, shifting your weight forward into a left bow stance. Your left hand comes back toward you as the fist is extended and stops with the palm facing the right elbow. *IMPORTANT POINTS:* The movement of the waist should follow the action of stepping. Keep the body upright to strengthen spinal energy. The right fist is clasped loosely. The right shoulder follows the direction of the fist, stretching forward. Keep your shoulders sunken and elbows flexible.

134

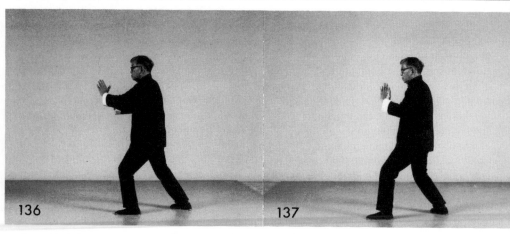

136

137

your hands out to the sides and down. (140) Continue to swing your hands down and then in toward your body as you step up with your right foot. *IMPORTANT POINTS:* The eyes are focused first on the two palms, then to the front. After the wrists join, the two hands should be separated. Elbows, after separation, should be kept beside the ribs so that *nei ching* (inner energy) is not dissipated.

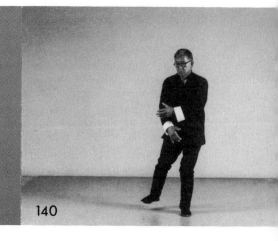

140

35

APPARENT CLOSE UP

(136) Slip your left hand palm up under your right elbow as you also open your right hand and turn it palm up. Slide your left hand forward under your right and bring it parallel to your right hand palm up. (137) Pull both hands over and back toward your body as you turn them palm forward and sit back on your right leg. (138) Push both palms forward as you shift your weight forward again into a left bow stance. Sit back again on your right leg and lift the toes of your left foot. (139) Pivot your left foot by the heel to point to the left, and shift your weight on your left leg as you separate

38

139

CROSS HANDS

(141) Place your right foot parallel with your left foot and about shoulder width apart from it. Meanwhile your hands swing upward in front of your body, your left hand crossing on the inside of your right. Both are palm inward. *IMPORTANT POINTS:* The arms maintain the form of two semi-circles crossed in front of the upper chest. Avoid any type of tension.

141

Continued

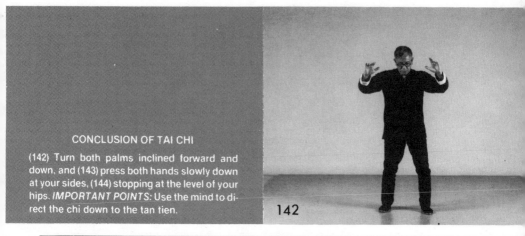

CONCLUSION OF TAI CHI

(142) Turn both palms inclined forward and down, and (143) press both hands slowly down at your sides, (144) stopping at the level of your hips. *IMPORTANT POINTS:* Use the mind to direct the chi down to the tan tien.

142

Contradiction and the resolution of contradiction is life. In the interplay of yin and yang flows the Tao.

—Wen Shan Huang

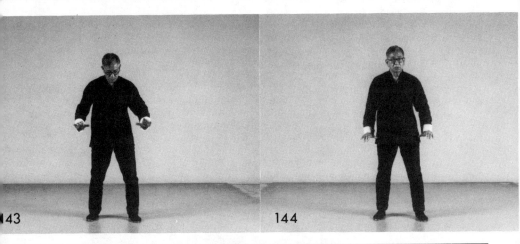

143 144

SELF-DEFENSE APPLICATIONS

Tai chi has proven to be unsurpassed as a great health exercise. Health exercise means a system of physical movement which nourishes human well-being. In commonly accepted terms, martial art means acquiring skills which fortify the well-being of the defender and which threatens the well-being of the aggressor should a confrontation occur.

Somehow there seems to be a physical and spiritual contradiction there. For many people however, there is not the slightest contradiction. Taking care of oneself is taking care of oneself. Life is simplified.

Tai chi, from the Chinese point of view, is historically a highly respected martial art, but it is difficult to attain proficiency without many, many years of intense training. What is the direction of that training? The focus is on developing a highly sensitive, flexible, quick-reflex, sinuous yet steely human entity who can use the aggressor's attack as a vehicle to a position of advantage, and who can then deal a punishing retaliation or a flight to safety.

Although the results of "push-hand" contests can be quite spectacular, tai chi is not a tournament art. It is based upon the principle of skillful yielding and defensive strategy. In the tai chi learning process, however, the postures and movements are often explained with combat rationale which can be imprinted with greater tenacity on human memory than abstract movements.

Incidentally, the few examples of applications depicted herein are quite elementary, easy to learn and demonstrate the possibilities.

COMMENCEMENT OF TAI CHI

(1) With feet shoulder width apart, (2) both hands are raised from their positions at the side of the body. (3) They are raised forward and up to (4) shoulder height.

SELF-DEFENSE APPLICATION: COMMENCEMENT OF TAI CHI

(1) The attacker approaches with both hands for the defender's neck. (2) The defender strikes with both hands under the attacker's arms, applying pressure to the nerve centers under his arms, causing pain.

PARTING THE WILD HORSE'S MANE

(1) From the hold ball gesture, (2) the body is shifted forward as the hands separate. (3&4)

3

2

3

Continued

The body shifts into a bow stance as the lead hand is extended forward and up while the other hand is lowered to the side.

4

2

WHITE STORK COOLS ITS WINGS

(1) The left hand is up and the right hand is down as the right leg steps out at an angle to the right. (2&3) The left hand comes down and the right hand goes up. As the left leg steps forward into (4&5) a left empty stance, the right hand is raised above the head and on the right side while the left hand is lowered to the left side at hip level.

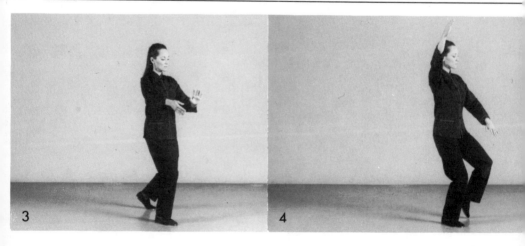

3

4

SELF-DEFENSE APPLICATION:
PARTING THE WILD HORSE'S MANE

(1) The attacker approaches from the left side.
(2) The defender wards off the attack by stepping into a left bow stance and pushes him off balance with her lead hand.

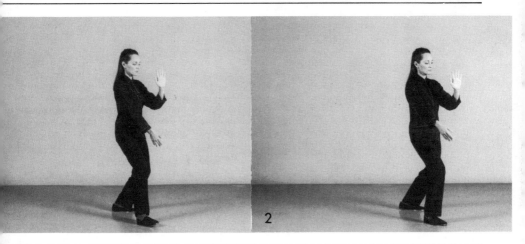

2

1

SELF-DEFENSE APPLICATION: WHITE STORK COOLS ITS WINGS

(1) The assailant attempts to grab the defender by the shoulder with his right hand. (2) The defender parries with her left hand as she steps in. (3&4) Then she strikes upward with her right arm under the attacker's upper arm to knock him back off balance, as her left hand comes down to the left side.

1

4

BRUSH KNEE

(1&2) As the left leg is raised, preliminary to stepping, the right hand circles down and back up behind the right ear and the left hand circles down to waist level. (3&4) The left foot steps forward. The right hand begins to press palm forward, and the left hand circles horizontally from left to right over the left knee. (5) The right palm presses forward as the left hand circles out to the left side, and the body is shifted forward into a left bow stance.

3

4

3

2

SELF-DEFENSE APPLICATION: BRUSH KNEE

(1) The defender blocks her assailant's left hand lunge punch by dropping her left hand down and back toward her toso. (2) In the same movement, she pushes forward with her right palm on his lead shoulder to prevent a follow-up with his other hand.

1

2

2

SINGLE WHIP

(1) With the right hand in the form of an eagle's beak, (2&3) the left hand sweeps across the tor-

PLAYING THE HARP

(1) With most of the body weight back on the right leg, (2) the left hand is extended upward and forward from the left hip to the front while the right hand drops down and back toward the body.

SELF-DEFENSE APPLICATION: PLAYING THE HARP

(1) As the attacker strikes, (2) the defender shifts back into an empty stance, parrying the blow downward with her right hand as her left hand comes up to deliver a strike to the throat.

1

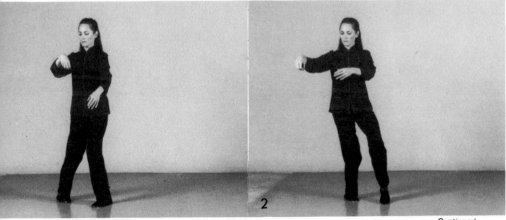

2

Continued

so and up while the body's weight is shifted to the right leg, and the eagle's beak is thrust out to the right side.

3

2

3

2

3

SELF-DEFENSE APPLICATION: SINGLE WHIP

(1) The attacker approaches with an attempted backhand strike for the defender's face. (2) The defender, using a right eagle's beak, deflects the strike, and in the same movement, shifts her weight toward him and (3) strikes to the face.

WAVE HANDS LIKE CLOUDS

(1) With the left hand up and the right hand down, (2) the left foot steps out to the left, and (3&4) as the body's weight is shifted to the left, the left hand begins to circle out to the left and down while the right begins moving upward in front of the body.

SELF-DEFENSE APPLICATION: WAVE HANDS LIKE CLOUDS

(1) To deflect the attacker's right punch to the face, the defender moves her body in toward the attacker's while her right hand executes the deflection, circling downward and to the right. (2) She steps in closer with her left foot and as her right hand pushes down, her left hand comes up to (3) deliver a strike to the attacker's face.

KICK WITH RIGHT FOOT

(1-3) Both hands circle down and in toward the body as the right leg is raised, knee flexed. The hands circle upward in front of the torso, and they overlap. (4-6) The right kick is accomplished by extending the foot after the knee is raised, while the hands sweep out to either side simultaneously.

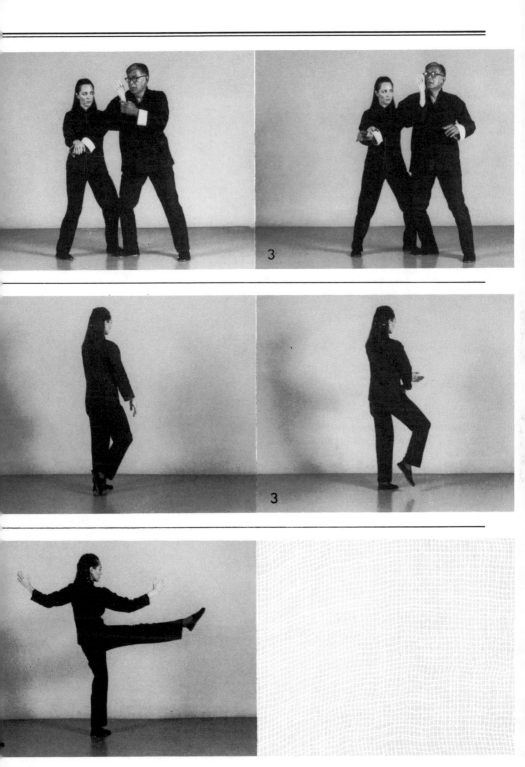

3

3

SELF-DEFENSE APPLICATION:
KICK WITH RIGHT FOOT

(1) The defender stops the attacker's advance with (2) a kick to the midsection using her right foot. At the same time, her hands spread apart, ready to block. (3) The defender turns to the right to face the attacker who then reaches forward to grab her. She uses her raised hands to block his hands.

NEEDLE AT SEA BOTTOM

(1-3) The right hand is lowered diagonally to a point about knee level directly in front of the centerline of the body. The back is kept straight and the bending is done by the knees and the hips. (4-6) Then the right hand is raised directly upward.

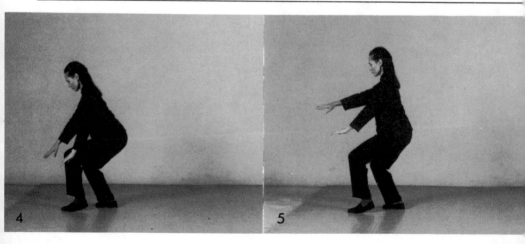

SELF-DEFENSE APPLICATION: NEEDLE AT SEA BOTTOM

(1) Confronted with an attacker who tries to control her with a wrist grab, (2) the defender drops her hand down low. This action breaks the attacker's hold. (3) With the same hand, the defender strikes upward to the attacker's face.

TURN AND CHOP WITH FIST

(1) With the body's weight on the left leg, the left hand raised, and the right fist in front of the center of the torso, (2) the right foot is pulled in toward the left, preliminary to stepping, the left hand circles out to the left side and down while the right fist circles upward in front of the body. (3) As the right foot steps out to the right, the body's weight is shifted forward, the right fist comes over and (4) chops downward as the left hand circles down and across the torso toward the front.

SELF-DEFENSE APPLICATION: TURN AND CHOP WITH FIST

(1) The attacker advances from the defender's right side, leading with his left hand as if to grab her by the shoulder. (2) The defender chops to the face with her right fist, striking downward with her knuckles as her left hand circles down and back. (3) The attacker keeps

2   3

2   3

1   2

Continued

circles down and back. (3) The attacker keeps coming however, and (4) he attempts a round-house punch for the defender's head. The defender blocks with her left hand, and finishes with a second strike to the face with her right.

3

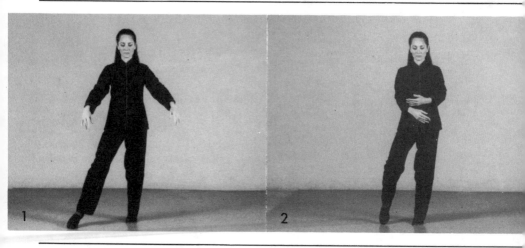

1

2

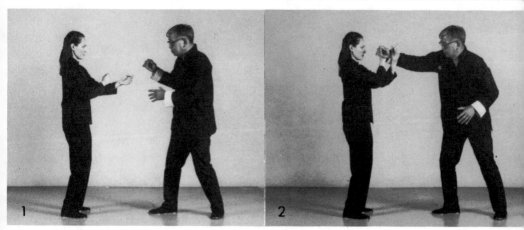

1

2

CROSS HANDS

(1) Circling downward on either side, both hands (2) sweep under and circle upward in front of the body as the right foot is pulled in toward the left. (3) The hands cross palms inward, the left hand on the inside of the right as they both come upward.

SELF-DEFENSE APPLICATION: CROSS HANDS

(1) The attacker strikes with a right hand lead. (2) The defender brings both hands under, crossing them, and deflecting the blow. (3) At the same time, she traps the attacker's wrist between her hands and gains control by applying a wristlock.

推手理

BASIC PUSH HANDS

Push hands is the name of a series of techniques wherein two persons test and train their sensitivity and ability to absorb, divert, or re-direct the physical energy projected by one or the other. This projection takes the action of a push, simulated strike, or a pull to subvert the other person's balance.

The reciprocal moves demand an alert but relaxed organism wherein the parts of the body alternate between assertion and reception until a position of advantage is achieved in order to uproot or throw the other.

Considering the objectives, the participants are, at the same time, partners and adversaries. The moving postures and positions are in constant change in reaction to ever more sensitive interplay and overt discharge of energy and force.

It is corporeal opportunism, dialectics, Taoism, psychological release, combat efficiency, and just plain good fun.

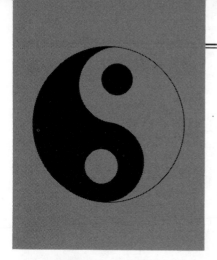

SINGLE HAND EXERCISE

The partner on the left is by the usual standards the weaker of the two, but in tai chi this makes little difference and in fact she may learn more from the push hands exercise as a result. If your partner is a woman as in this case, be aware that she, in fact, may have the advantage. She is forced to rely on principles rather than physical strength. (1) Face your partner and (2) bow to each other. (3) Step forward with your right foot, body weight on both legs as your partner does the same. Your right foot should line up and be parallel to your partner's and about ten inches apart. Extend you right hands palms facing inward so that the back of your hand contacts the back of your partner's. (4) As your partner pushes forward directly toward your chest to push you back, shift your weight back to absorb the force and at the same time, turn your torso to the right. Turn from the waist, and direct your partner's force away from your body to the right. Your partner's line of direction describes a curve. As your partner's hand swerves away from you, your hand rolls over from the palm inward position to the palm forward position. Then you (5) push forward by shifting forward and directing your force toward your partner's chest. Your partner absorbs your force by shifting back. Your partner then directs your force to the other side by turning at the waist. Your hand swerves out to the other side in a curve as your partner's hand rolls palm forward. Your partner then (6&7) pushes toward your chest once again,

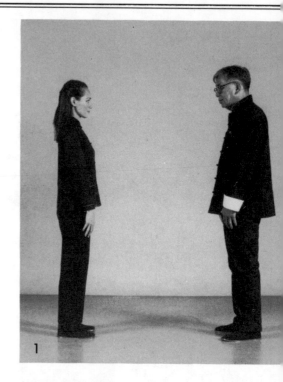

Continued

7

10

and the process (8-12) repeats itself again and again with both of you pushing and receiving in turn. Your hands never separate and the application of force is constant. You must advance when your partner retreats and vice versa. Both of your hands will move together in a horizontal circle.

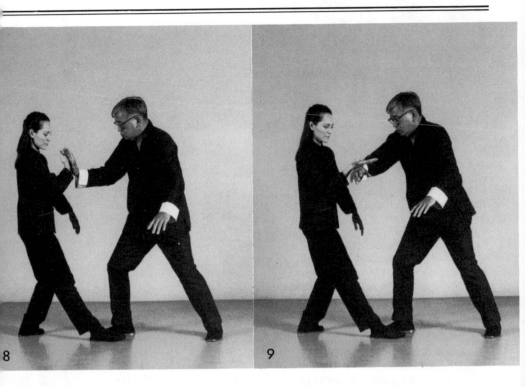

8

9

11

12

TWO HAND EXERCISE

(1) The foot positions are the same in this exercise as they were in the previous one. Again your right hands are extended so that the backs of your hands cross. Place your left hand on your partner's elbow as your partner does the same to you. (2) Turn your right hand palm forward and press forward with both hands, your right hand on the back of your partner's right hand, and your left hand on your partner's elbow. Your partner absorbs your pressing force by shifting back. Your partner then turns to the right and directs your force in that direction using both hands. Your partner's right hand rolls palm forward. Your partner then (3) presses forward in the same manner as if to lock your arm to your chest. You shift back to absorb the pressing force, drawing your partner's elbow toward you as you turn at the waist to re-direct the force to the right, (4) rolling your right hand palm forward, and the process (5-10) starts over again and repeats. The pattern of your movements with your partner is in a horizontal circle, and here again, as in all push hand exercises, the engagement of forces is unbroken.

1

4

7

8

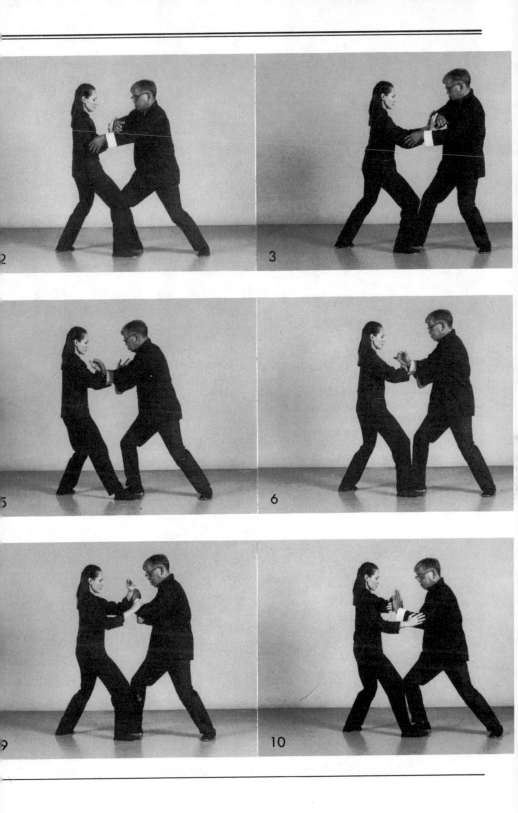

HEALTH BENEFITS OF THE FORMS

Each of the forms that comprise the eight-minute short form has internal applications as well which benefit the general health of the body and mind. The forms are listed here accompanied by a description of the healthful effects of the movements.

• *Commencement of Tai Chi:* This movement focuses the mind, causes relaxation, restores the internal systems and external muscles to their proper alignment, which in turn results in comfort. The chi breathing is harmonious, invigorating to the spirit, and tones the nervous system.

• *Parting the Wild Horse's Mane:* This invigorates the nervous system. It also strengthens the muscles of the face and neck, and improves circulation and the complexion of the skin.

• *White Stork Cools Its Wings:* This diagonal upright opening of the human figure extends and contracts the chest and back, toning the spinal nerves, uprighting the coccyx, and strengthening the alertness of the cerebrum.

• *Brush Knee:* This exercise contracts and strengthens the posterior muscles of the body. It also increases strength in the legs.

• *Playing the Harp:* The emphasis here is on training of the abdominal, waist, shoulder, and posterior muscles. It tremendously increases the extending and contracting strength of the two arms.

• *Repulse the Monkey:* The entire nervous system is benefited by this form. It also centers the spinal cord.

- *Grasp the Bird's Tail—Left* and *Grasp the Bird's Tail—Right:* These forms emphasize the splitting and enclosing of the limbs, and the contracting and expanding of muscles. They strengthen the muscles of the back and abdomen and help relieve constipation. The lungs are expanded and become strong, thereby helping to strengthen the heart. The legs and thighs are strengthened, and circulation is improved.

- *Single Whip:* This movement expands and contracts the joints, bones, and muscles of the hips and legs. It emphasizes split energy, and thus increases the flow of blood to the abdomen, improving digestion. The liver is invigorated, lungs expanded, and the knee and hip joints are made flexible.

- *Wave Hands Like Clouds:* The individual gains tranquility and calmness by the directed flow of energy from the *tan tien* (psychic center) to the whole body. Nerves are calmed, and the mind becomes peaceful and concentrated. Besides the reduction of excess weight in the waistline, it gives a general feeling of joyfulness and well-being.

- *High Pat On Horse:* This movement stimulates the *ching* (energy) of both arms, develops the chest, and improves posture.

- *Kick With Right Foot* and *Turn and Kick With Left Foot:* These forms increase the energy of the legs.

- *Strike Ears With Both Fists:* This makes the spine supple and elastic. It also strengthens the muscles of the arms.

- *Snake Creeps Down Left Side* and *Snake Creeps Down Right Side:* These increase the elasticity of the thighs and buttocks, and benefit the neck, shoulders, arms, thighs, knees, calves, ankles, back, and abdomen. They invigorate the whole system.

• *Golden Cockerel Stands On Left Leg* and *Golden Cockerel Stands On Right Leg:* These forms vigorously contract and strengthen the abdominal muscles, tone the spinal nerves and abdominal organs as a result of concentrating the center of gravity on one leg without wavering.

• *Work At Shuttles Both Sides:* This form relieves cramps and stiffness of the neck. It strengthens the entire chest and spinal area. The expansion of the legs and hands benefits those areas.

• *Needle At Sea Bottom:* The knees and the life force of the spinal cord are particularly benefited by this form.

• *Fan Through Back:* This form harmonizes the outer form of the body and stimulates the internal glands and organs. It trains the strength of the shoulders, back, and legs. It also develops the lungs, neck, arms, wrists, knees, calves, and ankles.

• *Turn and Chop With Fist:* This form reduces excess fat around the waist. It strengthens the waist as well as the thighs.

• *Step, Parry, and Punch:* The glandular functions are balanced. This form also strengthens the spinal column and the knee joints, and promotes flexibility of the hips.

• *Apparent Close-Up:* This form increases peristalsis of the bowels, invigorates the appetite, harmonizes gastric excretions. It also tones the spinal nerves and abdominal organs.

• *Cross Hands:* By vigorously stretching the arms, inhalation and exhalation are emphasized. The movements also tone the sympathetic nerves.

• *Conclusion of Tai Chi:* This form promotes the healthy flow of chi and concentrates the mind.